65p
UK Price

To THE millions of fans in Scotland who live, dream and eat football the 'Daily Record' brings a new feast of colour, drama and excitement.

In this, our second annual, you can live again the thrills of last season . . . look ahead into the rich promise of next year . . . learn what the biggest names in soccer think about the game you have helped make great.

The stories behind the stories in soccer from the men in the know . . . such names as Eddie Turnbull, Tom Wharton, Martin Buchan and Derek Johnstone tell you inside.

And the men who travel the world to report the big games, to meet the big names, are inside too . . . Hugh Taylor, Ken Gallacher and Alex Cameron let you into the secrets, the laughs . . . and the heartbreaks which make soccer supreme.

Our magic cameras have captured the action, the goals, the colour, the heroes which kept you talking and arguing and cheering.

Come inside, there's a lot to cheer about . . . it's a great book about a great game.

**Jack Adams
Sports Editor
'Daily Record'**

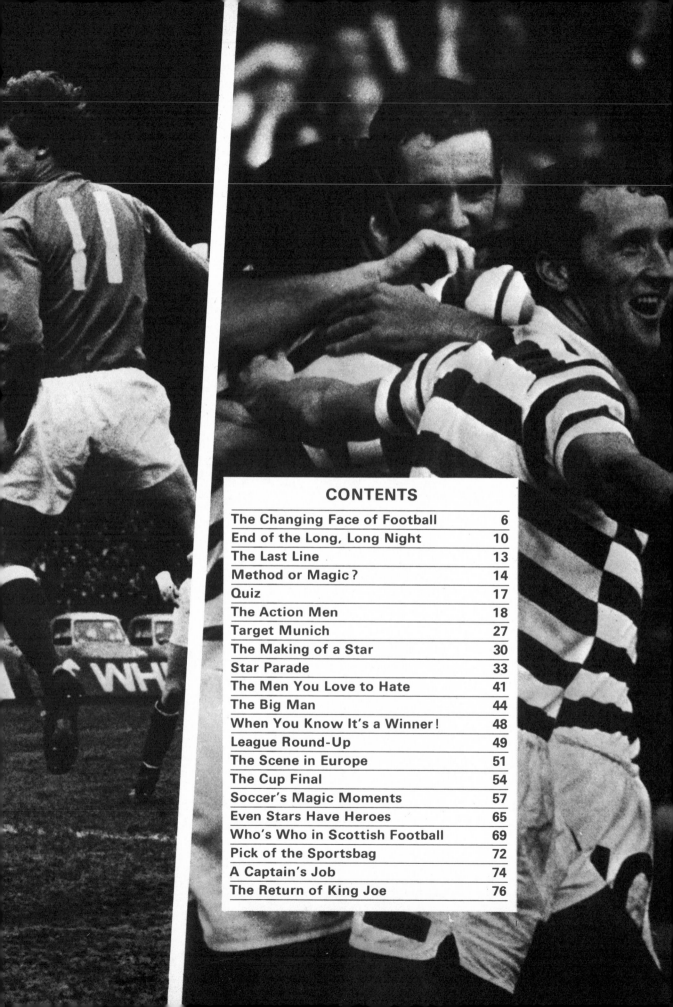

CONTENTS

THE CHANGING FACE OF FOOTBALL

FOOTBALL has changed dramatically in the past decade. The jet age has brought a new conception in style, torrid tournaments, substitutes, sponsorship, overriding control by team managers. Yet the sad feature for Scottish football is that, despite the football revolution, the attendances at most grounds are lower than they were 30 and 40 years ago.

Can we say, then, that football has improved? There is no doubt that the accent now is on method, willing workers and discipline, and when you see school teams trying to use a 4–2–4 formation, with sweepers and strikers and centre-backs, you realise there is no going back to the past — and what, to many of us, was much more entertaining, attractive soccer.

There are arguments that gates have declined because of a changing way of life, because of a more affluent society, giving the average man a more varied and luxurious choice of recreation.

I don't agree. I am militant in my view that while football has become a more exacting, more demanding game, with brainwork playing a bigger part in the numbers racket, the real beauty has gone out of the sport. In that I am backed by the great Alfredo di Stefano, of Real Madrid fame, who says football has become dull. Although technique, training and tactical plans have improved, di Stefano maintains, as I do, that there are fewer stars and too many teams are playing defensively.

The most depressing aspect, however, is that, to achieve success in modern football, you must fall in line and try to make the game an exact science. And when football becomes mass-produced, no matter how gleamingly perfect, much of the excitement vanishes.

What can be done to improve the image, to bring back the fans?

Celtic's example must be copied. They have played, in a drab age, football as explosive as any ever played in the past. They have kept gaiety in the game. And they have been the only Scottish club to find world acclaim.

But there is still too much emphasis on technique. And I think that, if ever Scotland are to lead the world again, the Celtic style must be tried at all levels.

Let's face it. Scotland are also-rans in the world stakes.

by Hugh Taylor

Power in the air . . . Motherwell inside-right Kirky Lawson hovers above Rangers defenders to bullet home a brilliant header

In the beginning we were not really champions of the world — for we *were* the world, we and England. Then, with the passage of time, we became, not the whole class but, at least, the top of the class, giving to an admiring globe a style of football that had poetry and fluidity and style.

Now, at international level, we are nowhere near the top. We have followed the dull lead of England, who won the World Cup with no special flair but with a dedication to method.

And I would not care if we weren't near the top if we had developed and specialised in an original style of football, perhaps temporarily in eclipse but sooner or later certain to dominate the world.

Alas, the classic players today are probably the Germans, and the great, attractive, acrobatic, graceful champions, the South Americans of Brazil.

Scotland head no particular school. We have no special style to offer to the world. Too many north of the border have copied English style.

This is all the more galling when you consider that Celtic did show that spectacular soccer, a splendid blend of the old and the new, could succeed in these grim, modern times.

Football used to be our birthright. I say too many in Scotland have become frightened, afraid that our naturally talented youngsters would be crucified in this age of the violent destroyer, and insisted that their teams play method football. The aim is not so much to win as not to lose.

And until this attitude changes I am afraid Scotland, as a footballing nation, will be looked on by the global elite in just the same way as Switzerland, France or Norway.

Yet there is one solution. Our league set-up is laughably out of date. Our divisions are too unwieldy. For years wise legislators have been crying out for reform. But that old frightened cry, "We must keep our place in the sun", by the small clubs has always stopped the formation of more workable leagues.

I am certain we would again be a great footballing country, with a style of our own, if there were three or four leagues . . . with no promotion or relegation for at least three years.

This would allow all clubs to set their own style, erase the fear of the drop to a lower division, and let football flourish again.

Now that sponsorship has been approved, there could be more competitions if the leagues were smaller, thus getting rid of the long, depressing grind in which, at most, only two or three clubs shine as title contenders.

The main problem, as I've said, is that while football has changed the crowds have withered.

This problem could also be solved quite simply — by playing the main matches on a Sunday afternoon. This, of course, will be greeted by cries of horror from the unco' guid and there will be many religious and traditional objections to it.

But are we any more religious than the people of the Continent who flock to matches on Sunday afternoons? After all, there is so much going on today on a Sunday in Scotland that I don't imagine an afternoon kick-off would do anything to disturb what sanctity of the Sabbath is left. There is plenty of time in the morning to attend church service, though, like the football grounds on a Saturday afternoon, the kirks are hardly packed.

And, with the shops closed, Sunday afternoon football would mean that more fans would be able to attend.

Well, the face of football has changed — but there has been little change in our way of thinking, too often Victorian. In this modern age, it is shocking to think that most of our ills could be cured simply.

For instance, there is no doubt the time has come to streamline the leagues — and also to consider amalgamation, in the form of country teams.

If clubs combined, they would be stronger, more able to provide a stern challenge to the giants. But can you imagine this ever happening; clubs such as Kilmarnock and Ayr United, Motherwell and Airdrie, Dundee and Dundee United getting together to form one unit in each city or county?

Maybe the time will come. After all, who ever thought football would see the day when firms poured money into the game, when there would be a British Cup?

Our real trouble is that while the face of football is changing, too many of us in Scotland are entering the jet age on a bicycle.

All-out power . . . Celtic's non-stop striker Willie Wallace flies goalwards with a flashing header

END OF THE LONG, LONG

FOR TWENTY-FOUR hours soccer babe Derek Johnstone shared a secret with his manager Willie Waddell . . . a secret that was to turn a practically unknown kid into a hero and start a new era for one of the most famous clubs in the world — Rangers.

The secret was that Johnstone, with only one game in the Ibrox first team, was to be in the Rangers League Cup final team to play Celtic at Hampden.

It was a gamble which shocked the 106,263 fans who turned up at Hampden . . . it was the move which brought sunshine days back to Rangers, which put an end to the long, long night during which Rangers hadn't won a major trophy in five years.

What a sizzling climax to a League Cup this game was to be — a League Cup that had already thrown up everything that was good about Scottish football.

In the quarter-finals Celtic had to play Dundee while Rangers faced Hibs . . . but already the fever was building up. The fans argued about the chances of an Old Firm final, and the result if there were one.

Dundee put up a great fight against Celtic in the first leg and drew 2–2 . . . but Hibs couldn't hold a Rangers team which was showing a new eagerness and hunger for success, and lost 3–1 at Easter Road.

The influence of Willie Waddell's youth policy at Ibrox was beginning to show, for those three goals came from teenagers Alfie Conn

and Graham Fyfe, who scored twice.

In the return games Dundee again fought bravely but lost 5–2 as Celtic took another step towards what they hoped would be their sixth League Cup in succession . . . and to prove that they had the young men to keep them at the top, young Lou Macari and Paul Wilson scored three goals between them.

Now, if Rangers and Celtic could keep apart in the draw for the semi-final, an Old Firm final seemed a certainty, for the other two teams in the last four were newly promoted Cowdenbeath and Dumbarton.

When the draw took place Celtic were drawn against Dumbarton and Rangers against Cowdenbeath . . .

NIGHT

Maybe it was the anger and insult of being written off, maybe it was just that old Cup magic which brings out real fighting spirit in a team, but both these little no-chance clubs got ready to show that Rangers and Celtic hadn't even started to fight for a place in the final.

And what a show they made of it . . .

Dumbarton went to Hampden to face Celtic. 30,000 fans turned up to see the goal-blitz that would surely blast the second division side out of the Cup!

What they did see shocked them, thrilled them, and sent them home with a new respect for second division

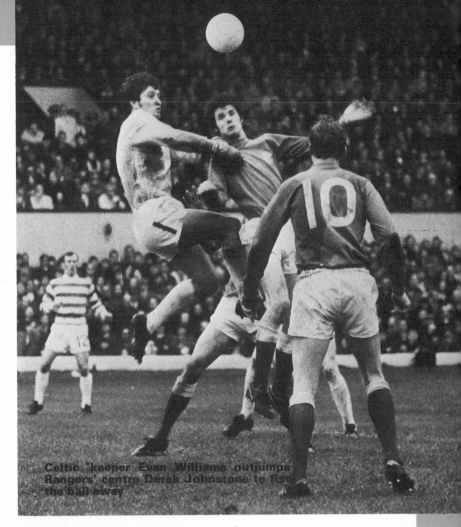

Celtic 'keeper Evan Williams outjumps Rangers' centre Derek Johnstone to fist the ball away

football. For these fighting Sons of the Rock held the mighty Celtic to a 0–0 draw . . . even after half an hour of extra time!

And, to crown a night of magic, their hero, goalkeeper Lawrie Williams, saved a penalty from Willie Wallace in the 114th minute.

The people who hadn't watched the game said it was a fluke result and looked forward to the replay the following week. It was impossible that these part-timers from Boghead could trouble Celtic again.

But Dumbarton are a team who are used to doing things the hard way . . . to do the impossible would just take them a little bit longer!

Rangers' left-half Colin Jackson rises above team-mate Derek Johnstone – but the ball flashed wide

The scoffers looked too right when Celtic raced away to a two-goal lead, both scored by Bobby Lennox, in the first 17 minutes of the replay.

Surely this would put out the fire that flared in every Dumbarton player? Surely Celtic would settle down to make up for that first game humiliation?

What did happen will be remembered as the greatest fightback of them all.

In 65 minutes ex-Celt Charlie Gallacher scored with a penalty and then Ken Wilson grabbed a well-deserved equaliser. Now Celtic were the struggling team . . . now they had to fight to survive.

Again the game went into extra-time and even the Celtic fans had to cheer this gallant Dumbarton team.

Celtic took over again and Willie Wallace and Lou Macari put them into a 4–2 lead with only 8 minutes to go . . . then, again, Dumbarton came back at them and Johnny Graham scored to make it 4–3.

But Dumbarton had run out of time and so, after 240 minutes of tremendous Cup football, Celtic had won a place in the final . . . and Dumbarton had won a place in the hearts of every soccer fan in Scotland.

In the second semi-final Cowdenbeath fought as bravely, but without the skill to beat Rangers, who won 2–0.

Now it was all set for the big one, the test between Celtic and Rangers . . . and the day of Derek Johnstone, a big, brave 16-year-old from Dundee.

As the 106,263 crowd swarmed into Hampden they argued about who the teams would consist of . . . very few of them guessed correctly! For the Rangers team announcement had two bombshells . . . John Greig, the Ibrox captain, was out because of illness, and Derek Johnstone, who had played only one full first team game, was in at centre.

Celtic were the favourites; in a poll of the other sixteen captains of Scotland's first division asking who they thought would win, the voting ended Celtic 13 — Rangers 3.

But on the eve of the match Willie Waddell had told Derek Johnstone that he would be in the team . . . then swore him to secrecy; even his mother and brothers were not to know.

The Rangers manager wanted Johnstone as a secret weapon, he wanted his heading ability to give the Ibrox attack more strength in the air . . . to the fans it seemed a gamble, to Waddell it was part of a plan.

And that plan paid off in 19 minutes when the 16-year-old centre outjumped the Celtic defence to brilliantly head home a great goal.

That goal settled Rangers, captained by centre-half Ron McKinnon. They started to play better football than they had produced for many years.

Their days in the soccer shadows were over, it was the end of a long, long night . . . Rangers had won their first trophy in five years, and a kid called Johnstone had become a hero.

Colin Stein looks on as Derek Johnstone outjumps Celtic's Billy McNeill and Jim Craig to head Rangers' winning goal in the 19th minute of the Cup

THE FUTURE of every club, the agony or ecstasy of every fan, depends on one man's split-second timing and bravery ... that man is soccer's last line of defence — THE GOALKEEPER.

The unsung hero of every team, yet the one who has to make the vital decisions, the decisions that either make or mar his team's performance.

Goalkeepers are a special calibre of player. Spectacular, athletic, lithe and agile, they're the men whose courage knows no bounds when it comes to answering the call of duty. Whether it's in the air or on the ground, it's all the same to the 'keeper. It's his duty to make that ball his ... he knows there is no place in the soccer world for the hesitant. A second of lost concentration will put his side in among the also-rans.

So let's take a close look at the men who make decisions for thousands, the men who walk a soccer tightrope every week ... the goalkeepers.

THE LAST LINE

Top: Evan Williams goes down at the feet of Ayr's Phil McGovern to smother the ball and prevent a certain goal.

Centre left: It's a Rangers' air-raid ... but Falkirk's Stewart Rennie fists the ball to safety and takes his side out of trouble.

Centre right: None but the brave! Denis Connagham of St Mirren takes the honours as he throws himself at the feet of Colin Jackson.

Left: It's all in the game ... when you're a 'keeper. Davie Stewart of Ayr United lays prostrate after a knock in clearing a shot from Joe Harper

THERE comes a time when most managers must make up their minds whether it is method or magic upon which their tactics and team will be based.

I certainly had to reach that decision a few years ago, and I had to reach it quickly, because relying on magic—on ball artistes as opposed to hard-working players — my Aberdeen team had slumped to a finishing position of fourth from the bottom in the Scottish First Division. It was then that I knew I had to make changes. I suppose I did it drastically. My ball players, the brilliant mid-field men Jimmy Smith and Tommy Craig, were sold. Smith went to Newcastle United for £100,000 and Craig moved on to Sheffied Wednesday for exactly the same fee.

From that season onwards I knew that I had to base my

Minutes to go in the 1970 Scottish Cup Final . . . Aberdeen manager Eddie Turnbull looks grim, but he's only minutes away from a 3–1 victory over Celtic

METHOD OR MAGIC?

main team plans on a method which would suit my players. It was too much to expect my team to be able to afford the luxury of ball players in the middle of the field who could do so many things with the ball . . . but very often needed someone else to win the ball for them. I admired the abilities of Jimmy and Tommy as much as anyone, but I knew that I could never play them together in the team. It was as simple as that.

It paid off for me, of course, because we won the Scottish Cup just a year later, then had our great League run last year. These

two successes came to the team because we worked hard at a system of play which we were certain would pay off. It was a system that we all believed in at Pittodrie.

Talk of 'method' football is often misunderstood in Scotland. People still tend to think of this term as meaning 'dull' or 'negative'. I have never agreed with this view and, certainly, our team at Aberdeen has been a team built to attack as often as possible.

We look on every man in the team as a potential attacker, including our captain and sweeper, Martin Buchan, and our centre-half, Tommy

by Eddie Turnbull, Manager of Aberdeen.

14

McMillan. All of them have the same message hammered out to them. If they see a gap opening up in the opposition line-up, then they go forward to take advantage of it. In a lot of teams you find defenders reluctant to go forward, even when it is right for them to do so. They fear that if the move they embark upon breaks down, then they will be left stranded up-field and out of position to the benefit of the other team. But what we look for from our players is that when one breaks, when a player does what we are looking to him to do, then another player automatically drops in to fill his position. This takes away the worry that players can have about responsibility for their own position.

You see, our set-up still has room for gifted players. Steve Murray is an exceptionally fine player, but we don't rely too much on any individual. When we had Craig and Smith we found that other teams were marking them tightly, tackling them hard, and biting quickly whenever they were in possession — which proved we were not functioning properly as a team.

Now it's not so easy for the opposition to upset our system by simply putting a couple of players out of the game. We have alternatives. We have variety . . . and this is what any good playing system must have.

This is another point we stress with our players at Pittodrie. We want them to be able to think for themselves when certain situations arise on the field. For instance, there can be times when we have discussed the opposing team and how we expect them to play and then they have changed their plans! All it needs is for an adjust-

Aberdeen skipper Martin Buchan (left) teams up with goalkeeper Bobby Clark to foil Kilmarnick inside-right Eddie Morrison

ment to be made by our players to sort things out. Sometimes it is easier for myself and my coach, Jimmy Bonthrone, to spot from off the field where things should be altered . . . but it gives me a tremendous kick when the players think for themselves without guidance. And this is happening now. We have players who are tactically aware of the situation which can exist in a game.

We have been fortunate in having some of the players with us for a considerable period of time; they have grown up with these ideas. Others, like Murray, right-back Henning Boel, and centre-forward Joe Harper, have fitted in admirably. You know, sometimes you can sense a little resentment from a new player when he comes to a club and begins what may amount to a re-education of the game. We had this kind of resentment from

man, and South American teams, seeing how they played and adapting to meet the new problems they posed for us. Now there is much more thought put into the game by managers and coaches, and the players benefit from the knowledge being passed on. Also, today's young player quickly grasps the messages he is given.

I see in my team the fruits of six years of work at Pittodrie, and I know that there is so much more to come because of the young players we have coming on. The great natural talents of Scotland are still blossoming, and I think we at Aberdeen get more than our fair share ... watch out for some of them inside the next few years. I promise you they will be good.

Joe Harper at the beginning. He wasn't too keen on the things we asked of him, but gradually he found that what we were advocating made him a better player. The resentment vanished. Joe is a wonderful player in tight situations in the penalty box ... but he is more than that — he has a natural football brain and is a particularly subtle player.

The system we have is a fluid one. I don't believe in rigidly applying a pattern on players when, in some cases, it might not suit their natural instincts. This is a mistake that is often made by coaches and managers. Players have to be comfortable in the roles they have assigned to them. A player in our team is always encouraged to use his initiative.

I think players today are generally better than when I was playing myself. They have better opportunities than we ever had. When I played for Hibs and for Scotland we used to work out tactics amongst ourselves. We learned by playing against the great Hungarian, West Ger-

Tempers flare (above) between Celtic 'keeper John Fallon and Aberdeen's Joe Harper. Joe shows his friendly side (below) as he hugs Alex Willoughby after a 3–0 win over Kilmarnock

QUIZ

Have a go at the quiz below — and see how much you know about the game!

PICTURE QUIZ

Here are six famous footballers of the recent past.

1. Ayr bought back their ex-centre-forward Alex Ingram from an English club last season. Can you name that club?
2. Which Scottish clubs play at: (a) Bayview (b) Central Park (c) Palmerston (d) Love Street (e) Somerset Park?
3. How many teams are there in the Scottish Second Division?
4. Which Scottish players have the nicknames (a) Jocky (b) Caesar (c) Dixie (d) Bud?
5. Which Scottish club did They all played in the international five-a-side sponsored tournament held at Meadowbank, Edinburgh,

Celtic goalkeeper Evan Williams previously play for?
6. Which Old Firm fullbacks were team-mates four seasons ago?
7. Which player competed in the European Cup with three different Scottish teams?
8. Which is the youngest League club in Scotland?
9. Where was the first soccer international played in Scotland?
10. Why is there an arc drawn outside the penalty area on a football pitch?

early in 1970.
Can you name them — and the countries they played for?

THE ACTION MEN

FALKIRK'S brave striker Alex Ferguson will never win any prizes for soccer elegance.

His hustling, bustling, sometimes awkward style might make the purist shudder.

But there can be no doubt that Fergie is an expert at the job he likes most ... scoring goals.

There are few players around who can be guaranteed to score at least 20 goals a season for their team.

Scottish defenders know there are very few ways of stopping Fergie when he gets a look at goal. Clyde 'keeper Tommy McCulloch shows one way – the illegal way – as Ferguson chases another goal

Fergie is one such player.

And there are plenty of thankful club managers and fans who can testify to the Glasgow man's goal-scoring ability.

Queen's Park and St. Johnstone enjoyed the sight of Fergie snatching goal after goal, but it wasn't until he joined Dunfermline that he really began to hit the high spots.

When Rangers, the team he always wanted to join, came along with a big bid it seemed that everything was perfect for Fergie.

But it didn't quite work out. And when Falkirk moved in with a £20,000 offer, they got their man two seasons ago.

It was a shrewd piece of business by Brockville's Willie Cunningham ...

For Fergie's goals helped them out of the second division ... then to a respectable place in the first division.

ALEX FERGUSON

SPEED, skill and a deadly shot ... that sums up the combined danger of Dundee's goal grabber supreme, Jocky Scott, the No. 1 Dens Park goal menace.

Scott, who had a spell at Chelsea shortly after leaving school seven years ago, is the man who carries a threat in his every route to goal. He has been one of Scotland's most consistent goal scorers over the past few seasons and has already received the honour as being ranked alongside that other prolific Dens Park striker Alan Gilzean, now of Spurs.

The Dens Park fans can pay him no higher tribute.

JOCKY SCOTT

WHAM . . . Scott slams a powerful header to Rennie's face

IAN TAYLOR

A SHREWD positional switch by Aberdeen boss Eddie Turnbull has resulted in the team losing a fair winger ... and gaining a top-class midfield player!

The man in question is Ian Taylor, who for five years had been on the fringe of things at Pittodrie.

Then last season, boss Turnbull decided to give Taylor a try in midfield ... and the answer was a new soccer discovery.

Taylor forced his way into the Don's cup-winning team, and is now a vital cog in the mid-line.

And the Pittodrie fans maintain that he is a player who must play for Scotland soon.

Midfield wonder Taylor leaves Airdrie 'keeper Roddy McKenzie and left-back George Caldwell standing in this great goal

19

RELIABLE . . . that is the word which best describes Rangers and Scotland centre-half Ronnie McKinnon.

Wherever the action is hottest . . . wherever the pressure is greatest . . . McKinnon will usually be found coolly marshalling his team-mates.

It is that assurance that has made him an Ibrox centre-half to rank with the greats. With the Woodburns and the Youngs.

Signed from Dunipace in 1958, McKinnon was soon impressing the Ibrox bosses with his play.

And when he did break into the first team . . . he was there to stay.

Perhaps his greatest moment came this season when he captained Rangers to their League Cup win at Hampden over great rivals Celtic.

Scotland fans, too, will be hoping that he and his new international partner Bobby Moncur, of Newcastle, can keep up the telepathic understanding they have struck up since they came together last season.

RONNIE McKINNON

Determination . . . Composure . . . McKinnon clears from the waiting Celtic forward Harry Hood in an Old Firm match

JOHN CONNOLLY

One of the most exciting sights in Scottish soccer... Connolly in full flight as he rounds a defender

THE ART of old-fashioned Scottish inside-forward skill is not dead. It is alive and well and living in Perth in the person of St. Johnstone's John Connolly.

Connolly is a newcomer to the Scottish soccer scene for he signed for Saints from Glasgow United in 1968.

But already he has won world-wide acclaim.

And his ability to make and take chances has already won him international recognition.

He was in the Scottish party that played against Austria in the World Cup qualifying match. And last season he won Under-23 recognition.

Already Britain's big-money clubs have been casting a jealous eye over this hottest of soccer properties.

This season there are sure to be more . . . if he maintains his current form.

CONTROVERSIAL...that's the only word to describe Ayr goal grabber George McLean, Scotland's man of many clubs.

You either love or hate McLean, but one things certain he's definitely one of the few characters left in Scottish football.

McLean burst into the soccer scene in 1961 when he played a major part in St. Mirren's Cup march to Hampden before they lost 2–0 to Rangers in the final.

He was a left-half then but already his powerful shot had been noted by many clubs and, in 1963, Rangers beat Celtic in a signing race for McLean. They signed him for £27,000 and it has been headlines all the way for big George since then.

He was Rangers' most consistent scorer in his four seasons at Ibrox, but the fans preferred to talk about the ones he missed rather than the ones he scored.

He went to Dundee from Rangers and again had the fans in two minds about his ability. From there he went to Dunfermline before Ayr United signed him for £12,000 last season, and now the Somerset Park fans are left to decide upon McLean's goal power.

But whether you're a McLean fan or not you've got to admit . . . he's certainly earned the title of a man of action!

GEORGE McLEAN

Arm upraised to the sky . . . George McLean shouts for joy as Quinton Young scores for Ayr in their shock 2–1 win at Somerset Park

KEVIN Hegarty, the raw youngster Falkirk said would never make it, took Scotland by storm in an avalanche of goals last season that has rocketed him to the top of the popularity polls with the Hearts fans.

He's agile, fast and has got lots of guts. Where others would hesitate, Hegarty the Brave would charge in and, more often than not, get one of the impossible goals that he has become famous for.

At the start of last season Hegarty was an unknown . . . after only a handful of games his name was on the tongues of soccer fans everywhere — especially at Parkhead!

For, in two League Cup section games against Celtic, Hegarty scored three goals . . . and his soccer dream was now a distinct reality.

Anyone who saw Hegarty score the second of his two goals at Parkhead will never forget that particular 'impossible' goal.

A low cross from the left wing was heading towards either Celtic's Billy McNeill or George Connelly . . . but in one swift second Hegarty dived between to send an 18-yard header crashing past Evan Williams into the net.

That goal is typical of Hegarty — and there's plenty more where that came from.

NOW WITH EAST FIFE.

KEVIN HEGARTY

Goal! Kevin Hegarty soars above Dunfermline wing-half Jim Fraser to bullet home a brilliant header

SOCCER fans on Tayside certainly know how they like their game. They say that they can tell a good 'un from a bad 'un by his first kick of the ball . . . and one man they are unitedly agreed upon as a good 'un is Dundee United's skilful left-half, Jim Henry.

Henry, a powerful, ball-playing mid-field man, shows the maturity and class of a player who has been in the game for years . . . yet long-haired Jim has been a regular at Tannadice for only three short seasons.

A master of the through ball, Jim has now donned the mantle as United's answer to his old rival Jimmy Smith, the ex-Aberdeen man who went to Newcastle for £100,000 two years ago.

Smith and Henry are very alike in character and style . . . but the Tannadice fans are sure he has one more valuable asset over his £100,000 counterpart — *he can tackle!*

And you don't have to be a Tayside fan to realise if you've got a blend of artistry and power then you've definitely got a good 'un.

JIM HENRY

Dundee's exciting left-half discovery Jim Henry launches a powerful tackle on Celtic's right-back Jim Craig

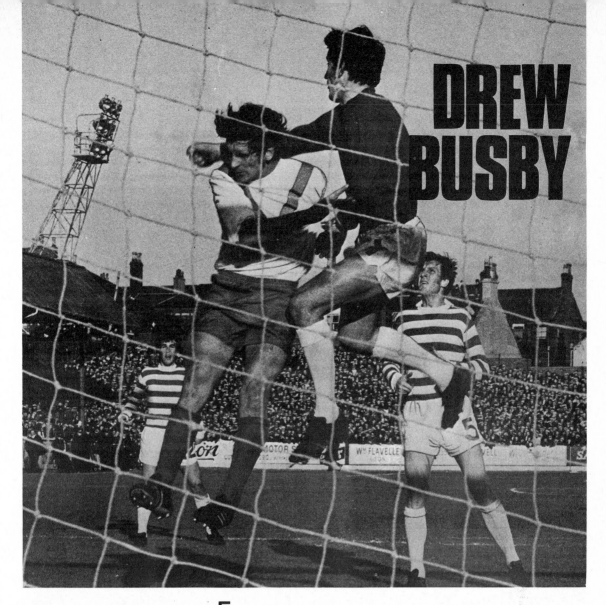

DREW BUSBY

Airdrie's Drew Busby challenges Celtic 'keeper Evan Williams to a high ball

Ever since striker supreme Drew Busby exploded upon the Scottish football world, Airdrie fans have been doubting the ability of talent-spotters on both sides of the border.

And with little wonder! Busby had actually been *freed* by three clubs — Coventry, Third Lanark and Partick Thistle — before finally taking a last chance gamble as a soccer senior with Airdrie.

His gamble paid off in no uncertain fashion. He rocketed to the top of the scoring charts and became menace No. 1 to clubs everywhere.

In a fantastic goal burst in his opening 13 games last season, Drew crashed home 14 goals and almost single-handedly K.O.'d mighty Nottingham Forest from the Texaco Cup with four goals over the two legs.

His effect on the Broomfield side has been amazing. His courage and power has given the Broomfield men tremendous confidence and the Airdrie management insist he is *not* for sale . . . at any price!

Changed days for Drew, the goal machine who became a cast-off from three clubs and has now proved them all wrong!

ONE MAN the word action might have been invented for is Celtic's non-stop winger John Hughes, a man who has thrilled soccer fans throughout the world.

The Parkhead fans insist if you haven't watched Hughes in full-flight then you've never really lived. Head down, ball at the feet and an explosive finish . . . these are the powerful assets of Celtic's human hurricane.

Hughes emerged on the scene as a raw centre-forward in 1960 . . . but even then his ability was never doubted.

He took the punishment that came his way, brushed it aside and continued to be a top performer in grounds everywhere in the soccer world.

Before Jock Stein arrived from Hibs as Celtic manager in 1965, Hughes had his moments, but like many other temperamental stars, he lacked consistency.

Hughes is now a mature European star and has settled down well at outside-left.

The dynamic giant, nicknamed the 'Bear' by the Celtic fans, has found the touch that separates the genius from the average.

JOHN HUGHES

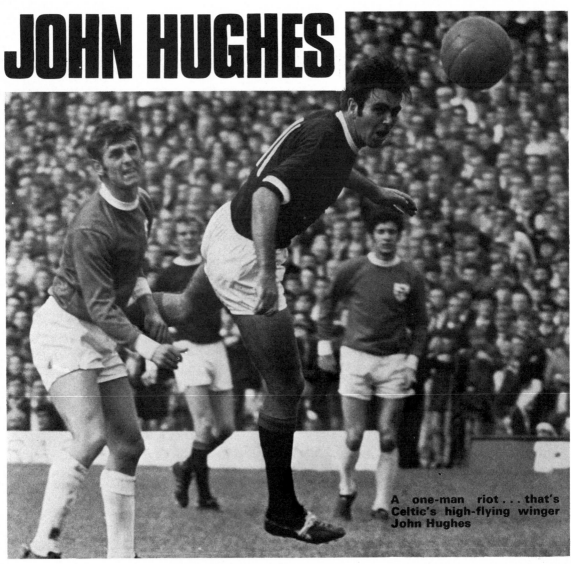

A one-man riot . . . that's Celtic's high-flying winger John Hughes

TARGET MUNICH

THE World Cup finals have always been a special occasion in soccer . . . a competition with an aura of its own, a competition of unchallenged and unapproachable glamour.

And the next World Cup finals, which promise to be the most spectacular, the most thrilling ever seen, are approaching fast.

From Scotland to Scandinavia, from Wales to West Germany, countries have already begun to lay their plans for success at Munich '74.

And in Scotland, like most other countries, the emphasis will be on the young front to provide the stars who will become household names in 1974 . . . names like West Germany's Muller, master of goals in Mexico . . . names like Jairzinho, the Brazilian with the scoring flair . . . names like Cubillas, the Peruvian who scored such wonderful goals.

These men went to Mexico already heroes in their own country. They went home as world class stars in the eyes of millions of soccer fans.

Is there a Muller in Scotland . . . a Jairzinho . . . a Cubillas?

Certainly in a season that had its share of disappointments nationally and internationally, there were bright young hopes discovered who could become stars in Munich.

For instance, one of the greatest nights of the season was back in dark February, when the pride of England's Under-23 players came north . . . and were desperately lucky to escape with a draw.

It was a night of discovery for the Scottish fans. A night when they realised the little-known players from our provincial clubs could not only hold their own with the big-money boys from the south . . . but could teach them a trick or two.

The Englishmen had in their side the biggest cash buy in the history of British soccer — Colin Todd, transferred only days before from Sunderland to Derby County for £170,000.

He was overshadowed by Hibs' John Blackley.

The English had Alan Hudson of Chelsea, the boy who nearly made it to Mexico with England's senior team.

Peter Lorimer . . . Leeds' powerful Scots striker

27

He was overshadowed by Airdrie's Drew Jarvie, a Coatbridge motor mechanic.

The English had Ray Clemence in goal, a young man Liverpool boss Bill Shankly had been raving about.

But until he was injured, Motherwell's Keith MacRae, who had interrupted a journalism course in Edinburgh to play, had looked a better 'keeper.

It is to the MacRaes, the Jarvies, and the Blackleys that we must look if we are to succeed in Germany.

And there are many, many more youngsters to make up the team in Germany . . . and before.

For every team — even some in the second division, which is at least showing an improvement in techniques, class and ability — has its young stars.

Hibs, as well as the cool, composed Blackley, have in Arthur Duncan another young man who was a success that cold wintry night in February against the English giants.

And they also have a wonderful wing prospect in an even younger player — Kenny Davidson — of whom boss Dave Ewing thought so highly that he played him against the might of Liverpool in the Fairs Cup.

Hibs lost . . . but Davidson showed he had the nerve and the skill for the big occasion.

Another Davidson, this time Celtic's Vic Davidson, is a future star who could be in Scotland's side in the next year or two, and with him there could be two teammates at Parkhead — George Connelly and Davie Hay.

Connelly, the man for all positions that manager Jock Stein appears to be grooming for centre-half, and Hay, the complete professional in his

Kenny Davidson . . . the 18-year-old starlet for Hibernian

approach to the game, could be vital men when it comes to Munich '74.

Rangers, like Celtic, have their young stars. Youngsters like Alfie Conn, famous son of a famous father who plays with the maturity of a senior member of the team, and speedy Sandy Jardine, who broke through completely to hold a regular place in the Ibrox first team last season.

But the time seems to

have gone when the big two had the lion's share of the talent.

For there is the challenge of the brave men of the north and, Aberdeen, last season, spotlighted the class of Dons' skipper Martin Buchan, Scotland's youngest skipper — and one of the most successful.

The challenge spotlighted the goal-snatching ability of wandered Joe Harper, who after two spells with Morton and one down south with Huddersfield, found goal glory with the Dons.

And Hearts, although they fared poorly in the league and Cup, played solidly in defence, where full-backs Davie Clunie and Peter Oliver played excellently. And they began to play youth cap Eric Carruthers as the season progressed, and cashed in with goals.

But the biggest eye-opener of the season was the sparkling form of the real provincials, the teams who are never mentioned in the same breath as Rangers or Celtic, Hibs, or Hearts.

For their youngsters showed they, too, can be Munich marvels.

Tom Forsyth, a whole-hearted gutsy Motherwell player who didn't know if he was better in the back four or mid-field, proved he could be brilliant in both . . . Cutty Young, the boy from Rabbie Burns country, took time off from his miner's job to produce some wonderful displays on Ayr United's right wing. . . . St Johnstone's John Connolly continued to progress as Perth fans hoped he would . . . and into the Saints' team came a young man who has modelled himself on Connolly, youth cap Jim Pearson.

Of course, no Scottish team will be chosen without anglos, as there are some brilliant youngsters in the south.

Leeds' Eddie Gray had an unfortunate season with injuries, but he is one of the men around whom a Scottish team will be chosen in the future, while Blackpool's Tony Green, pushed into the Scottish team for the second-half of the Liège disaster, has shown many promising touches.

And, also fighting his way back as the season ended was Peter Marinello of Arsenal, the babe who went south as the new George Best . . . and couldn't live up to his own special publicity.

When you remember about kids like that other London hero Eddie Kelly, or Leeds' Peter Lorimer, you can see Scotland can still be a hit in the competition that has brought them nothing but heartache.

This is the tournament in which Scotland have 'won' the reputation as good losers. . . .

Beaten in the qualifying stages by West Germany, . . . beaten by Italy, who although fancied, crashed out of the 1966 section which included little North Korea, and beaten by Czechoslovakia, who finished runners-up.

It is not a good record.

It is up to the youngsters who make up the brave new world of Scottish soccer to put it right.

Archie Gemmell of Derby County looks hopeful . . .

THE MAKING OF A STAR

IN THE glamorous world of big-time soccer, stars are made, not born . . . and no-one knows this better than the young man who made the biggest impact on Scottish soccer in season 1970–71 . . . Derek Johnstone of Rangers.

When sixteen-year-old Johnstone nodded Rangers to their first major home success in four years in last season's League Cup final against Celtic at Hampden, he won himself instant recognition . . . but not instant stardom.

Young Derek is the first to admit that he has a long road to travel before he fully deserves the acclaim which was showered on his young head after his golden goal.

Like some of his famous Scottish predecessors, Derek has outstanding potential. Denis Law, John White, Alan Gilzean, Dave Mackay, Jim Baxter, Billy McNeill and his club-mate Willie Henderson all had that potential, that little bit of star quality, as teenagers.

But it still took all of these famous soccer Scots a year or two to realise their potential. All of these players had that little piece of soccer magic in their make-up which, in time, elevated each one of them to the lofty role of soccer idol.

But it still took muscle-aching hours of training, coaching and practice, and then more of the same, to win them that place in the limelight of big-time football that every player waits years for.

Derek Johnstone knows full well that he, too, must endure all these things if he is to scale the soccer heights . . . and that is exactly what young Derek means to do.

Like most famous football Scots, the teenager Ranger has been 'fitba-daft' ever since he was big enough to toddle.

From the age of five young Derek was never off the streets of his home town Dundee, kicking a ball about with the rest of his young pals until their impatient parents finally chased them indoors.

But it was not until Derek reached the age of eleven that he played in organised football, and took the first faltering steps which led to his goal of a lifetime at Hampden.

It was then that the star potential, which prompted Rangers to sign Derek, finally shone through. He was a star in his own right at Fintry Primary School, Dundee and, by the time he reached Linlathen Secondary School, his promise had been spotted by Scotland's schoolboy international selectors.

By the age of fifteen Derek had helped Scotland to the international schools championship by scoring in consecutive matches against Wales, Ireland and England . . . performances which had the top clubs on both sides

by Bob Patience

Rangers' golden boy Derek Johnstone is out of luck this time as he goes for the ball with Billy McNeill. Celtic goalkeeper Evan Williams clashed with both of them

of the border clamouring for his signature.

It was here that fortune smiled on Rangers and scowled at his boyhood favourites Dundee United. United asked Derek along to Tannadice with a view to signing, but Derek did not fancy the Tannadice set-up and, shortly after, plumped for Rangers.

The Ibrox backroom man who recognised that young Derek could be a star-in-the-making was Rangers' Dundee scout, Tommy Gray . . . he is the man Rangers fans can partly thank for that long awaited League Cup win.

And it took Derek only one day at Ibrox to realise

that he would have to push his young body to the extreme if he was to gain the glory that he dreamed of.

Derek says: "The first few months were really tough going. It was great to be amongst players such as Willie Henderson, Ronnie McKinnon, John Greig and Colin Stein but it didn't take me long to find out that physically I was far from ready.

"I started along with other boys as ground staff with the usual tasks of cleaning up after the older players and going through all the training routines.

"The training at first was really murder. I used to go home to Dundee with my

muscles aching after morning and afternoon sessions at Ibrox. But gradually I got used to it all, and now I actually look forward to these daily training sessions. However, I soon found out that being a professional footballer was not as easy as everyone thinks."

These daily sessions have moulded Johnstone into one of Scotland's most promising young men. His aerial ability was quickly noticed by Rangers' boss Willie Waddell and, helped by coach Jock Wallace and his assistant Stan Anderson, the tall, dark-haired Dundee youngster is fast improving his ground work too.

"Jock Wallace and Stan Anderson have been tremendous help for me," says Derek.

"I've still got a long way to go yet but I feel my play, both on the ground and in the air, has improved enormously under them.

"There is a lot of interest taken in we young ones at Ibrox and that is very encouraging. And of course we are allowed to train with the first team pool all the time, and this helps our confidence immensely. We feel part of Rangers' plans right from the start and so, when we do get our first team chance, we are prepared for it."

Johnstone got his chance early. He was still only sixteen when manager Waddell put him in against Cowdenbeath in a League match at Ibrox . . . and Derek promptly helped himself to two goals in a fine debut.

Says Derek: "It was great to get these goals and I will always remember them, but really it was the other more experienced lads who helped me in that game. I was a bit nervous at the start but they helped me along, encouraging me all the way, and I think they enjoyed my goals as much as I did myself."

Johnstone is still surprised at the rapidity of his climb to the first team. He says: "I never thought I would get my chance so quickly. I was surprised to get that game against Cowdenbeath, but it proved to me that I had made the right choice between Rangers and Dundee United."

A few months later Johnstone scored a goal against Celtic that every Rangers fan will never forget, and the career of a prospective star was well and truly launched.

Now a regular first team spot is Derek's big aim. "Naturally I want as many honours out of the game as possible – I would love to play for Scotland for instance – but my big aim is to do well for Rangers. They have

Derek Johnstone holds the League Cup in triumph

been great to me and I want to do everything I can for them. I hope that Celtic goal was only the first of many in matches of that type.

"But I'm prepared to wait for my chance. I know Rangers are doing the right thing by me . . . now it is up to myself."

Ability, ambition and attitude are all there for Johnstone. His League Cup final goal against Celtic opened the gateway to soccer stardom. When he finally bustles his way through it all, the hard work and coaching will be well worthwhile . . . a star will be made!

Jim Craig and Billy McNeill look back in anguish as Johnstone's header eludes the outstretched arm of Evan Williams

Kenny Aird, St Johnstone

Steve Murray, Aberdeen

Joe Mason, Morton

Hugh Robertson, Dunfermline

THE MEN YOU LOVE TO HATE

by Tom (Tiny) Wharton

It's all in a day's work for a referee. Here referee McBain of Bankhead books Motherwell outside-left Brian Heron for a foul on Rangers' Willie Henderson

WHEN I go to work on Saturday afternoons I carry three watches, a pencil, a wee black book and a coin or coloured disc.

I have to run from eight to ten miles, during which I'm guaranteed the doubtful privilege of upsetting a lot of people.

In case you don't know . . . I'm a referee. One of the men who adjudicates each week before crowds who vary sharply in numbers and temperament, but who rarely agree completely with the man in the middle.

I know I'm a man many love to hate, although I like to think that, off the pitch, as well as on it, I get along with people who believe in keeping on the right side of the law.

Let me tell you about my hobby from the inside – I emphasise *hobby* because I certainly don't do it for the money!

Referees are the type of men who are used to making decisions. They have to be or they would never be any good. There is no time in the middle of a Cup Final or the lowliest league match to stop and ponder over whether or not a penalty is called for.

Referees aim at winning the respect of the players and officials. They don't want to be popular, but ask only to be acknowledged as knowing their business and applying fair decisions.

I cannot emphasise too strongly that a referee must have no bias of any sort. It's difficult but essential.

Sensible players and officials — and most of them are! — recognise that a referee has to make decisions and it's inevitable that they won't all be in their team's favour.

Football is becoming more and more of a technical game. The good players are entitled to feel they are protected by the laws of the game which, of course, have to be implemented by men like myself.

Don't get the idea it's all serious. At some of the smaller grounds the spectators can be really funny and sometimes there's even a bit of banter between the players and the men on the terracing.

But, even in this convivial atmosphere, we always have to remember that no game is more important than another. However, some matches *demand* more than others.

The most difficult match to handle is, of course, between Celtic and Rangers. The stress which is put on a referee in the 90 minutes of an Old Firm game doesn't apply in any other match.

Don't let anybody kid you, *this* is the greatest club match of all — but it brings

Tom 'Tiny' Wharton displays the paraphernalia of refereeing

Biographical detail: Wharton is 44, 6ft. 4in. and 17st. Began refereeing in 1946 and was rapidly promoted to Grade 1. Handled International and European matches and is recognised as one of the best referees in world soccer.

tremendous tensions with it.

Referees are very conscious of the electric atmosphere and the danger of repercussions which can follow any of their decisions in a Rangers/Celtic match. And at the same time they know that there are no special football laws which apply to Old Firm games.

The handling of these matches calls for a lot of diplomacy. It also requires the players of both teams to be on their best behaviour!

Another problem is the noise. It's fantastic! When I come off the park my head is usually thumping. But the noise is just a distant rumbling. Referees have no time to pick out rival chants or anything of that sort. At smaller grounds they can hear what individual fans are saying – "Get a white stick, ref!" and that sort of thing.

But during an Old Firm match a referee hears nothing but noise . . . and more noise.

Referees cannot allow themselves to be distracted. Refereeing, in fact, is the one hobby I know of in which a man forgets his job completely.

Could you imagine a referee being successful if he was thinking about how to get his next contract when, in the same instant, he was required to make a decision about a penalty?

I think business executives should think twice about taking up refereeing. I'm serious. If they play golf, for instance, they go round talking about business. Well, I can assure you that the minute I go on the pitch I forget about everything. There is enough for any human being to concentrate on during 90 minutes of football.

A referee should have a sense of humour. Very often if people shout unfriendly things and the referee laughs it off, the abuse soon stops.

The most exciting stadium I've been in during my world travels was the Maracana in Brazil. A huge bowl which holds 200,000. I refereed when Wales and Chile played there . . . and it was a really wonderful experience!

I couldn't believe my eyes when I saw the star players going over to TV and radio commentators at half-time and giving lengthy interviews about the match. Each star seemed to have his own channel! It took about half an hour to get them back on the field after the interval!

Seeing the atmosphere and the goings on at grounds like this has made me feel that it's time we, in Scotland, stopped catering for what I call the LCD – lowest common denominator.

You won't hear me knocking this great game of ours in any way, but I do feel it's time fans paid more and were given greater comfort in return.

Over the years people have made jokes about my bulk. But I've never considered it a disadvantage – in fact it is an advantage, especially when it comes to controlling an angry six-foot player. My height gives me a good view at reasonable distance and if I go too close it could present a problem for the players breaking out with the ball. Once or twice in important matches I've had to go much closer than I would have liked. I've stepped between players to stop them fighting. This is not a course I'd recommend to every referee but when you're as big as I am then it can be done with the right results.

It's all part of the job.

Referee Thomson of Edinburgh upsets St Johnstone by allowing a goal to Celtic's Willie Wallace. Saints players follow him in protest, but the ref's word is final . . . decisions, decisions

THE BIG MAN

THE LOUNGE of the hotel at Harrogate was hushed as the Big Man began his tactics talk. Carefully he held up the marker with the number seven on it and told his players: "This is where we can win the game. Wee Jimmy can win it for us . . ."

The Big Man, Jock Stein, manager of Celtic, was talking about his right-wing soccer genius, Jimmy Johnstone, on the eve of the European Cup semi-final first leg against Leeds United, in the spring of 1970. Of course, Celtic won that game at Elland Road 1–0, and then won the Hampden return 2–1 to reach the European Cup final for the second time. In each game Jimmy Johnstone, just as Stein had said, was the outstanding Celtic player, leaving the highly rated Terry Cooper stranded time after time.

It was an outstanding tactical victory for Stein, and the story of Johnstone and the tactics talk is now forming part of the soccer legend that the Big Man — the players' name for him — has seen grow around him since he took over as manager of Celtic early in 1965. He is the kind of man legends and stories must grow around. His stature and his record demand them.

When Tommy Docherty used to joke: "I get the Glasgow papers sent down to London and the Prime Minister is on the back page and big Jock's on the front,"

he wasn't far from the truth. For Stein has been the outstanding soccer figure in Scotland since he moved to Celtic Park as manager. In fact he is probably the greatest football personality this country has ever produced.

You have only to travel abroad with him to see the recognition he has gained in every soccer country. In Italy he would command a huge salary if he ever decided to join the soccer rat-race there.

Juventus and other leading Italian clubs have long been interested, but Stein prefers to stay in Scotland . . . and to stay with his beloved Celtic. I can remember one Italian sports writer in Florence, who told me after a fine Celtic performance: "We would give anything to have such a manager as Mr Stein here in Italy. Always we have defence, defence, defence because the coaches are afraid to try anything else. But Stein he is a man who likes to attack. He could save our football . . ."

Basically that Italian summed up the finest attribute that Stein has shown as a coach. He has refused to defend except on very rare occasions. One of them he remembers with a shudder even today some five years later. Celtic went to Prague to meet Dukla in the European Cup semi-final second leg. They had a two goal lead to defend and they did it by subduing the natural instincts of the players and hanging on to the lead at all

costs.

Says Stein: "It was a terrible display we gave that day. We were so keen to get to the final, to be the first British team there, that we we went completely into defence. I don't like to think back to that game now. I would never do it again. Sure, I'll go abroad for games and tighten things up a little, but never will I retreat the way we did in Prague. I like to have the chance of getting goals away from home and I have tactics with that in mind when we go abroad today."

He has been the greatest advocate of attacking play in modern football. Always he has stressed that his players want to attack, that the natural way for them to play is to go forward.

There is no more exciting sight in soccer than a Celtic team being taken off the leash in a home leg of a European Cup tie. A Celtic team going for goals is the way the fans like to see them.

Yet Stein, and his talents for tactics and for handling players, were almost lost to football. He walked out on Albion Rovers, his first Scottish club, after a resigning dispute and moved to non-League football in Llanelly. He played there forgotten, until someone at Celtic Park remembered him as a big, raw centre-half who was possibly the man to solve a temporary centre-half problem which had hit the club.

And so Stein returned to

by Ken Gallacher

**Stein at the top . . . Celtic's world-famous mana-
ger Jock Stein stands proudly with right-half
Bobby Murdoch after Celtic's magnificent 2–1
win over Inter Milan in the European Cup Final
in 1967**

Scotland for a fee of £1,000 or so, and he remembers now how he stood outside the ground on his first morning, watching the established stars go in, and wondered: "What am I doing here?"

It must, indeed, have seemed like a dream. The tall ex-miner coming back home to Scotland to play with one of the most famous teams in the country. Yet there was more to follow.

Celtic manager Jimmy McGrory made Stein the captain of the team . . . and the qualities of leadership had been recognised for the first time. Stein skippered the team which won the Coronation Cup in 1953, the team which did the League and Scottish Cup double in 1954. It was around this time, too, that the interest in the tactical side of the game began to grow.

He saw the great Hungarians destroy England at Wembley and he watched them again in Switzerland for the 1954 World Cup. He

One of Jock's 'retreats' from the pressures of the soccer world is being out on the golf course.

still enthuses over players such as Boszik, Puskas and Hidegkuti and keeps a film at home of their match against England at Wembley.

He says: "That team taught me so much about the game. I can still watch that film and marvel at some of the things that they did then. They were

Jock shows who's boss as he 'send's off' Bobby Murdoch in a practice match. Well, he was playing for the other side!

A master tactician . . . one of the best managers in soccer . . . but when it comes to a training session you'll invariably find Stein stuck in goal.

all great players and they had a system working for them at a time when every team in Britain was still playing it off the cuff."

These Hungarians influenced the young Stein in his ideas. Ideas which he put into practice first of all as a coach at Celtic Park when his own career was prematurely ended because of an ankle injury — it still troubles him occasionally today. Among the youngsters he was in charge of then were Billy McNeill, who became Celtic captain, and Pat Crerand, who moved on to Manchester United. Crerand remains a Stein disciple, never hesitating to tell any doubters south of the border: "The Big Man is only the best there is. He's fantastic. The great thing about him, too, is that he never asks a player to do anything that he isn't capable of doing. Everything is geared to the natural ability of the player and he never forces players

into systems . . . his systems fit the players. They are not contrived, they're natural."

Stein moved on to become manager of Dunfermline . . . and dutifully won the Scottish Cup. He moved again to Hibs . . . and won the Summer Cup. Then came the move to Celtic and a collection of trophies that will probably never be equalled. In five years at Celtic Park he has won the Scottish Cup three times; the League titles five successive times; the League Cup five times and in Europe, had won the European Cup; been beaten finalists in the same tournament and reached the semi-final of the European Cup Winners' Cup.

It is the finest managerial record of any manager, at any time, in Britain. I am convinced that it will stay that way, too.

Yet there is no mystique about Stein and his success. He doesn't talk about football in high-flown phrases,

his conversation isn't littered with the coaching jargon that so many managers use. He stays straight-forward, blunt and detests the mumbojumbo that so often surrounds the role of a manager. When people talk to him about the strain he must be under, he snorts: "Look, everyone in every job is under strain. A bus driver is under strain every minute of his working day just the same as me. I don't go for that talk. Strain isn't an exclusive problem for football managers."

It is this down-to-earth attitude that keeps him close to the huge Celtic support. It is probably that same attitude that has kept him at Celtic Park although he could have moved on to other clubs several times. Stein has a loyalty to Celtic and he has spent his time as manager repaying the club which brought him back from the wilderness of Wales. The debt has been settled.

WHEN YOU KNOW IT'S A WINNER!

WEEK in, week out, football fans throughout Scotland — all over the world, for that matter — flock to soccer grounds everywhere following their favourite teams. But from Glasgow to Milan, from Ibrox to the magnificent San Bernabeau in Spain, they all have one aim in common . . . the fans are there to see goals, goals . . . and more goals. Their explosive terracing reactions are typified in the joy of the goal scorer. If the fans like to see them, then the players certainly love to score them.

Here are some of the strikers' reactions when they answer the fans' endless cry . . . the cry for goals.

Yippee! It's a great feeling! Hibs' Arthur Duncan shows his elation after scoring against Hearts

THE MEN WHO MADE HISTORY

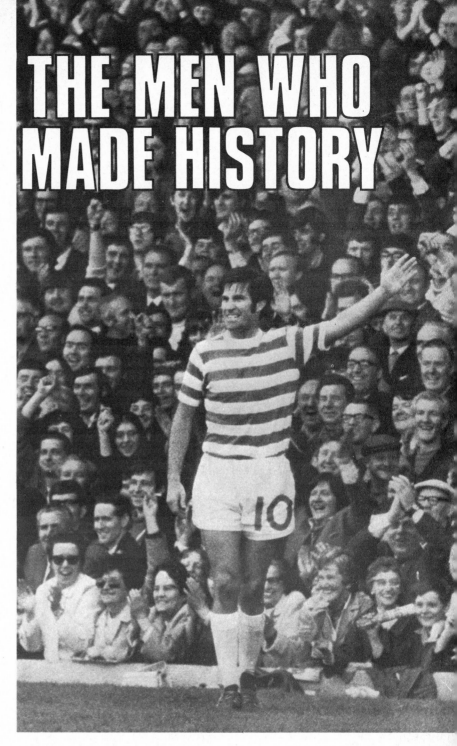

IT WAS a day to remember, a day Hollywood would have found hard to surpass for drama, nostalgia . . . or plain old-fashioned magic.

Any one of the 30,000 fans who turned up at Parkhead on the first day in May, 1971 will remember that this was much more than the last league game of the season between Celtic and Clyde.

It was the end of a football fairytale and the promise of a new era for the club who had conquered Europe and made a million friends with their gay, goal-drenched style of play.

For this was the last bow, the final curtain call for the eleven men who had so proudly earned the title of the Lions of Lisbon when they won the European Cup . . . never again would those heroes play as a team in competitive football.

Never again would the loudspeakers boom out the magic names . . . Simpson, Craig, Gemmell, Murdoch, McNeill, Clark, Johnstone, Wallace, Chalmers, Lennox, and Auld.

Jock Stein, the giant behind the fabulous football machine had wanted it this way, he had wanted the fans to get a final chance to cheer the men who had given them so much to cheer about in the previous six years . . . six years that will almost certainly never be repeated.

Two nights earlier Celtic, without some of those men of magic, had won their sixth league title in as many years by beating Ayr United 2-0 at Hampden.

But what a sizzling battle it had been to clinch that history making sixth league flag after a tense, season long battle with Aberdeen.

Aberdeen had started quietly with a home draw

Bertie Auld waves a proud farewell to the Parkhead crowd

with Airdrie. But after they lost 2-0 to Morton at Cappielow on October 3, 1970 they hit a tremendous run.

IN FACT THEY WON FIFTEEN GAMES ON THE TROT . . . and their goalkeeper, Bobby Clark, set up a European record by going 12 games without losing a goal.

They won two golden points by beating Celtic 1-0 at Parkhead.

And even with the season only half gone it was already a two horse race . . . with Aberdeen setting the pace.

The deciding game looked set for Pittodrie on April 17 as both teams struggled to keep up the tremendous standards they had set.

First one faltered, then the other . . . but they were still the only two candidates for the title, at least ten points ahead of the third and fourth teams St Johnstone and Rangers.

The big showdown at Pittodrie lived up to all the ballyhoo and build-up it had received.

Both teams forgot about the tensions and turned on a match fit to decide any championship . . . but it ended in a draw 1-1.

Now Aberdeen had to face Falkirk in their final game, Celtic had three games left against Ayr United, St Mirren and Clyde.

Then, with their final fling came disaster for Aberdeen when Falkirk beat them 1-0 thanks to a penalty by the Bairns captain George Miller.

It had been a brave fight by a great team . . . but now it seemed to have all been for nothing.

For Celtic's game that day was postponed . . . leaving the Parkhead side needing only three points from their last three games to make sure of the title on better goal difference.

Still the excitement, the drama, the tension wasn't over, for Celtic decided to play their last games in the same week, and the first would be against St Mirren.

Harry Hood shows his joy after scoring against Aberdeen

What a climax; St Mirren needed both points to avoid relegation and put Dunfermline down into the Second Division . . . but Celtic couldn't afford to be kind.

St Mirren showed they asked no favours by twice grabbing the lead, but twice Celtic fought back to draw . . . and sent these fighting Saints along with Cowdenbeath into Division Two with Partick Thistle and East Fife winning promotion.

Celtic finally wrapped up the league by beating Ayr at Hampden.

Now the time was right, the stage set for Jock Stein to pay his tribute to the eleven men who had given Celtic it's greatest moment in those six great years.

And what a farewell those Lions of Lisbon made it by slamming in six goals to beat Clyde 6-1 . . . it was certainly a day to remember, and a team to remember!

A tearful Bertie Auld is carried off by his team-mates

THE BIG TEST...

THE REAL test for a player, a club, or a country that wishes to flex its soccer muscles, that wishes to find out if it is really as good as it thinks it is comes in the red hot furnace of European competition.

It is in these games, the European Cup, Cup Winners' Cup, the Fairs Cup and the European Nations Cup that the big test comes . . . it is out of this football furnace that the real iron men come, the real winners.

Scottish players and clubs have known the bitterness and frustration of defeat in Europe, but they have also won the praise, drunk the heady wine of success . . . and it is the thirst for more success

that every year sets our top clubs and players chasing a dream, a dream of European glory. Last season it was again Celtic who led that challenge determined to wipe out the haunting memory of the previous year's final when they lost to Feyenoord.

The Parkhead side made a blistering start beating the unknown Kokkola from Finland 9-0 at home then boosting their aggregate to 14-0 with a five goal win away from home.

Celtic's luck was in, for in the next round they were drawn against little Waterford from Ireland and this time they rattled in ten goals over the two games to go into the quarter finals on a

10-2 aggregate.

Now there were no rabbits left, no easy games . . . and Celtic ran up against a double Dutch disaster when they were drawn against Feyenoord's great rivals Ajax.

Celtic's dream of revenge and glory died in Amsterdam when Ajax caught them on a bad night and crashed in three goals. The Parkhead boys got ready to fight for their soccer lives in the second leg at Hampden, but this time courage wasn't enough and although Celtic won 1-0 they were out of Europe for another season.

And with Celtic went the last hope of the sad Scottish fans who had watched our teams crack one by one

Vic Davidson (left) hits the post with the Kokkola defence completely helpless

under the tremendous pressure of the challenge in Europe.

In the Cup Winners' Cup Aberdeen made a great start with a brave 3-1 home win over the famous Hungarian side Honved . . . but Budapest and the return game was entirely different.

The Dons lost 3-1 and with the aggregate locked at 4-4 the Scots had to face the nightmarish tension of deciding the tie by penalty kicks.

Steve Murray took the first and scored, then the Hungarians scored with theirs, Joe Harper scored, they equalised, Jim Hermiston scored, they equalised, Alex Willoughby scored . . . and again they equalised.

Now it was Jim Forrest's turn . . . and his shot hit the bar and stayed out. The man who stepped up to take Honved's vital fifth was their 'keeper Koscei and he made no mistake to make the Hungarians 9-8 winners.

Unfortunately not all our teams can claim that they made such a brave show.

In the Fairs Cup the all-seeing microscope of first class competition again found the flaws and weakness that spell defeat and failure in the chase for a place in the soccer sun in Europe.

Rangers lasted only one round . . . but they could claim that they had drawn one of the top teams in the competition, Bayern Munich, with the deadly double act of World Cup stars Muller and Beckenbauer as brilliant as ever.

The Ibrox side lost 1-0 in Germany and despite a great fight in the second leg they could only draw 1-1 . . . all their vast experience on the soccer battlefield of Europe had gone for nothing again.

Our other three challengers Kilmarnock, Hibs, and Dundee Utd. were soon to find out just how tough a testing ground Europe was to be.

Kilmarnock can count the tourney as a disaster. They got what seemed an easy draw against Colrains . . . but the Irish side were not. They held Kilmarnock to a 1-1 draw in Ireland . . . then shattered the Scots by winning 3-2 at Rugby Park.

So another Scots side learned the sad, stinging lesson that there are few easy teams in the biggest test of them all.

Dundee Utd. started off with a 3-2 home win against Zurich Grasshoppers and entered the second round by holding the Swiss team to a goalless draw in Zurich . . . again it was a good start, but again it was to end in failure.

Sparta Prague brought the Tannadice boys up to date with the soccer facts of life by beating them 3-1 in Prague. This was too much for the game United side to pull back so although they won 1-0 at home they were also out.

Hibs were to be the last hopes . . . so the soccer spotlight switched to Easter Road. Europe and it's glamour, excitement and tension were nothing new to this famous club.

Hadn't they been the first British side to play in the European Cup?

They opened their bid for glory with a crushing 6-0

Jimmy Johnstone hurdles Ajax 'keeper Stuy as his shot flies for the net . . .

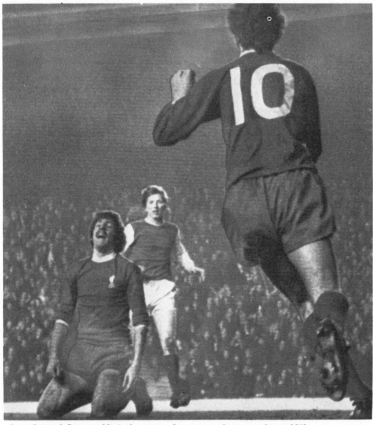

An elated Steve Heighway after scoring against Hibs

those two goals were enough to take Hibs through for Guimares could only pull one back in the second leg in Portugal.

Now the temperature was rising, the opposition getting hotter and in the next round Hibs were drawn against those magic men from Merseyside, Liverpool.

Liverpool were going through a rebuilding stage with their team, the great names of the past were slipping out, Ian St John, Ron Yeats, Tom Lawrence. New names were taking over in the never-ending battle for the headlines. Names that at that time meant little to the Scots fans, names such as Larry Lloyd, John Toshack, Steve Heighway.

And there was still the King of the Kop, the man who had taken Liverpool out of the soccer slums and turned them into one of the most respected clubs in the world.

That man was Bill Shankly who nursed his Scottish pride and kept it warm with a blanket of success, who wore his Scottish accent like the badge of some elite, exclusive club.

That man hated the word defeat, he hated losing to his own stars in five-shillings-a-head practice matches.

That man made sure that his new young lions had that same grim, frightening determination to win . . . and win they did.

At Easter Road Hibs couldn't raise their game enough and went down 1-0 . . . in the second leg they lost 2-0.

The challenge was over . . . but the dream was still alive, there was always next season, Europe would still be there to be conquered.

win over Malmo at Easter Road and in the return leg in Sweden scored another three to win 3-2 and 9-2 on aggregate.

Round two threw Hibs in against Vittoria Guimares of Portugal. At home the Scots won 2-0 despite wasting a lot of good goal chances that don't come too often in this grade of football. But

Rangers' Alex Macdonald outjumps the Bayern defence . . .

WEE JIMMY'S

THEY called it 'The Jimmy Johnstone Spectacular'. Its official title was the Scottish Cup Final. A gala occasion between the world's greatest rivals — Celtic and Rangers.

It was in this spectacular setting, a tense Wednesday night at Hampden on May 12, a dramatic, frenzy-filled replay in front of over 100,000 fans that Jimmy Johnstone, Scotland's biggest problem child, decided to come of age. To put his rare talent on view for the world to see. And the applause was deafening . . .

In typical Johnstone fashion he kicked off the Cup campaign in an indifferent note when Celtic cantered to a 5-1 first round victory over Second Division Queen of the South at Parkhead.

Over at Ibrox Rangers raced to a 3-0 win against Falkirk and followed this up with a good 3-1 win over St Mirren at Love Street in the second round.

Celtic faltered a bit at this hurdle — drawing 1-1 at Parkhead against Dunfermline — but they made up for it with a solid 1-0 victory in the replay at East End Park. Harry Hood was the scorer.

In the quarter-finals it was Rangers who stuttered a bit against the challenge of Aberdeen at Ibrox. The Dons sealed their goal and with 'keeper Bobby Clark in magnificent form it seemed almost certain to go to a replay at Pittodrie the following Wednesday.

Then, in one fatal split-second of indecision, the Dons' Cup hopes were shattered in the 76th minute when Colin Jackson followed up a corner-kick to force home the only goal of the game.

Celtic had no such problems in their match and

SPECTACULAR...

raced to a 7-1 victory against Raith Rovers at Parkhead.

Celtic, Rangers, Hibs and Airdrie went into the semi-final draw.

A brilliant solo goal from Willie Henderson put Rangers ahead . . . only for a superb run and cross Alex Cropley to leave Jim O'Rourke an easy chance to equalise two minutes later.

Both teams slugged away, fought a nerve-racking battle late into the second-half until 14 minutes from time when young Alfie Conn crashed home a close-range winner.

This had been a fantastic tussle, a match for men . . . but everyone knew now that the best was yet to come.

May 8 heralded yet another clash of the Titans, the greatest club match on Earth . . . Celtic v Rangers

A joyous Lou Macari after scoring for Celtic

in the Cup Final at Hampden.

Rangers, depleted by injuries to stalwarts such as Sandy Jardine, Davie Smith and Alfie Conn, were confident of winning their 20th Scottish Cup.

Celtic, also hampered by injuries and loss of form to Bobby Murdoch, Tommy Gemmell and John Hughes, were certain of winning their 21st Scottish Cup.

As usual the atmosphere was raw with excitement when skippers Billy McNeill and John Greig led their teams on to sun-drenched Hampden with a crowd of 120,000 sending volumes of sound echoing round the ground.

But it was in this hectic atmosphere that a frantic, hurried and desperate dive into a fairy-tale saved Rangers from defeat.

Trailing 1-0 to a goal from Bobby Lennox just before half-time, Ibrox boss Willie Waddell took a last gasp gamble and sent on substitute 17-year-old Derek Johnstone for Andy Penman with 30 minutes to go.

With only 3 minutes left it looked as if fairy tales only happen once in Cup Finals. Celtic were still leading 1-0 and the Cup was halfway to Parkhead. Then in stepped Derek Johnstone.

A long ball from Willie Johnston suddenly had the Celtic defence in panic and as goalkeeper Evan Williams and sweeper George Connelly hesitated, in popped Johnstone to nod home a slow-motion goal. It was his first Scottish Cup-tie!

Mystery surrounded the Ibrox squad as they prepared for the replay. Their injury jinx had struck again when young right-back Alex Miller, himself a replacement for Jardine, had to go off with a broken jaw.

Who would get the problem spot was an Ibrox secret up until kick-off time on Wednesday. The place went to young Jim Denny, a wing-half from Yoker making his debut after only a handful of reserve games.

Celtic brought in Lou Macari for Willie Wallace. But it was only too obvious right from the start as to who the master of Hampden was . . . Jimmy Johnstone.

A jinking, darting, devastating display from Johnstone had the Celtic fans in ecstasy. He was a menace

by Alex Gordon

55

when he decided to stick to his wing, he was a danger when he played across the park and he had the Ibrox support in a tangled mass of nerves with his every touch of the ball.

In the 24th minute, after a spell of Rangers pressure, Celtic took the lead with an unbelievably simple goal. Bobby Lennox swung over a low corner from the left, Billy McNeill dummied it and there was Lou Macari lurking only 6 yards out to whip the ball into the net.

The Celtic fans erupted in a joyous sea of green and white as the Rangers legions stood in disbelief.

One minute later another tidal wave of green and white went from the Parkhead faithful . . . Celtic had scored again!

A mix-up on the edge of the Rangers penalty area saw Tommy Callaghan push the ball into the tracks of the inrushing Jimmy Johnstone and a last ditch tackle from Ronnie McKinnon brought the wee Celtic wizard crashing to the turf. A penalty! Referee Tiny Wharton pointed to the spot as a deadly hush swept through Hampden.

Harry Hood, looking the calmest man on the park, strode up confidently and crashed a low shot into the net.

Rangers rallied after this crunching, moral-sapping double blow but it looked too late. Again Waddell sent on Derek Johnstone in the second half for Penman and unbelievably he had a hand in Rangers' solitary goal, scored shortly after the interval.

John Greig swept over a cross from the right, Johnstone worked his way between Tommy Callaghan and Billy McNeill and slipped a close-in shot under Evan Williams's diving body. Jim Craig appeared on the goal line but, under pressure, his misdirected clearance went into his own net.

Rangers saw hope, their fans were suddenly filled with a new life . . . but in stepped Jimmy Johnstone to interrupt their dreams. He took it upon himself to take over the command of Celtic and his magic footwork had Rangers reeling once again. Unstoppable and unbeatable, wee Jimmy made the ball his own possession as he tricked, teased and tortured the Ibrox men.

The final score was 2-1 for Celtic, giving them their 21st Scottish Cup triumph... but more important was the birth of a man who can lead Scotland out of their soccer wilderness.

The headlines summed it up best . . . 'The Jimmy Johnstone Spectacular'.

All smiles for Celtic after their 21st Cup win . . .

It's congratulations all the way from his delighted team-mates after Kilmarnock centre Ross Mackie scores against local rival Ayr United

It's danger for Morton's defence as Celtic inside man
Harry Hood makes a quick breakaway

Kilmarnock's Jim Cook shows how to beat a defensive wall as he crashes in a free kick past Ayr United at Somerset Park

Dundee United left-half Jim Henry is just too late to stop Celtic's George Connelly getting in a shot

Celtic 'keeper Evan Williams bravely cuts out a cross to rob Rangers' centre Colin Stein of a great scoring chance

Celtic's John Hughes in full flight, ready to shoot at goal, as a Dundee player moves in behind

Falkirk 'keeper Stewart Rennie safely clutches a high ball as Rangers' centre Colin Stein gets up to challenge

Manchester City goalkeeper Joe Corrigan makes a one-handed save as Celtic inside-left Bobby Lennox rushes in during a pre-season friendly match.

EVEN STARS HAVE HEROES

THEY are as much a part of the soccer scene as a corner-flag or a penalty kick, and sometimes they are welcomed . . . sometimes they are not!

Yet where would football be without kids, the youthful fans who crowd round club entrances or team coaches in the hope of getting a closer glimpse of their idols?

The reward for a long wait may be just a quick word, or perhaps an autograph for the lucky ones whose book, or just a scrap of paper, is thrust forward into the star's hands.

And back in the fans' homes the giant-sized pictures of the players they idolise probably gaze down at them from thousands of bedroom walls.

Kids are part of the continuing interest in the soccer scene which the sport must maintain if it is to keep its position as the number one spectator sport.

They can be a nuisance sometimes – by needlessly running on to pitches to hail goals – but if they give up, then the supply of fans which has kept football in

Willie Henderson's hero . . . Stanley Matthews.

that top spot for so long would soon dry up.

Every boy who has ever kicked a ball identifies himself with a star he has seen . . . even if the player is only the dashing centre of the local amateur side, or a household name such as Georgie Best.

Yet the idols of today were once in the same position as the kids of today, starry-eyed youngsters who dreamed of football fame.

Who were their heroes? . . . whose footsteps did they want to follow? We've asked a few of them — we think you might find their answers surprising.

Take Scotland 'keeper Jim Cruickshank. Maybe you thought the Hearts man spent his childhood studying the technique of the world famous 'keepers of the late fifties, before he joined his first senior club, Queens Park.

Not a bit of it! Jim's heroes were the great middle-distance runners of the time, and especially the ones from behind the Iron Curtain.

He explained: "I did not become a 'keeper until I was about 13 or 14, so it was never a position which interested me that much.

"And I did not concentrate on footballers, for the men I really admired were these athletes."

So he thrilled to the heroic exploits of the famous Czech, Emil Zatopek, and the Russian, Vladimir Kuts.

And he still says: "For the sheer guts they showed in some of their wonderful races I don't suppose professional footballers could lick their boots

Hearts 'keeper Jim Cruickshank — athletes were his heroes

The star he worshipped as a kid . . . Emil Zatopek, the Czech runner

"It's the individual effort that's required in these punishing races which impressed me then, and still does. There's no-one to help you; an athlete is so completely on his own."

We also found out that so many of the youngsters whose names are known all over the country today were so busy playing football themselves that they hardly had time to watch the stars.

But so long as they could nip along to a game they were ready to watch football, at any grade.

So for the youthful Bobby Murdoch his first idol did not come from the Celtic side so successfully captained by the man who is now his manager, Jock Stein.

As a youngster his first spectating was done at the junior ground nearest his home of Rutherglen Glencairn . . . and Bobby fancied himself following their centre of those days, Harry Hurrell.

"He was the man who scored the goals, and I suppose for all kids that's the most glamorous role," he said.

The first Celtic player he ever studied closely was the late Joe Baillie, and Bobby was eventually to slot into the same mid-field role.

"He was the first player whose picture I ever bought," said Bobby.

But it was TV, and the 1954 World Cup which gave Murdoch a team whose example he felt he wanted to copy.

"Like all youngsters I saw the game in the simplest of terms. But it was that year I began to realise there might be more to the game than just bashing the ball upfield and hoping to score.

"I saw some of it on television, and I remember I was heart-broken when the

Ferenc Puskas (above), the Hungarian legend who became one of Bobby Murdoch's first boyhood idols

Hungarians were beaten in the final.

"That was the team of Puskas and company, what an attack-minded side they were, I suppose one of the best-ever."

Some players, of course, saw themselves mentally operating in the role which, later on in life, they were to fill successfully.

So for the tiny Willie Henderson, from that famous Airdrie schools nursery, there was never any other position but the right-wing, no other jersey he wanted to pull on, but the number seven.

And just as thousands of would-be soccer stars today imagine, as they dribble round school playgrounds, that they are Willie Hender-

son, so, for the little Rangers star — and all the budding right-wingers of his time — there was only one player to try to emulate — Sir Stanley Matthews.

The role of television is so normal to today's kids that they accept it with the commonplace attitude they have to space flights.

But for nine-year-old Willie Henderson it was a wonderful thrill to see one of the first-ever televised Cup Finals, the Coronation Year epic between Blackpool and Bolton Wanderers.

Those were the days when there was perhaps only one television set in each street — hard to realise today — and as neighbours crowded round the set wee Willie was one of them who watched that dazzling performance from Matthews.

A performance etched forever on the minds of those who saw it, which swung the Cup to Blackpool, and gave Sir Stanley his first, and only, F.A. Cup-Winners' Medal.

And for Willie, years later, came the realisation of a dream he had nurtured ever since that day . . . when he played in Stanley Matthews' benefit game.

He said: "He was fifty then, but he still had the touches that had made him great. It was incredible . . . for after all, at that age, most people can't even run for a bus."

Henderson was just one of a host of world stars who had travelled to Stoke for a match which was filled with nostalgia. For these great players, just as starry-eyed as any youngsters, carried Matthews off the field shoulder-high at the end.

One of the great veterans of today's soccer scene, and a man who is still an idol to millions, is Manchester United's Bobby Charlton.

For Aberdeen's Jim Forrest it was Charlton whom he most admired — a star whose career started as a headline-maker in the fifties, stretched right through the sixties and now into the seventies.

"When I was at school Bobby Charlton was a winger, and I never really fancied myself in that position," said Jim.

"I was a centre then, although when I went to Ibrox, the trainer at Rangers, then Davie Kinnear, always said the wing was my best position.

"However it was years later at Aberdeen that I became a winger, and of course, by that time Bobby Charlton had long since moved into mid-field.

"He is such an accomplished footballer in any position, but it was those electrifying bursts down the wing which used to thrill me.

"Actually I spent a week at Old Trafford training with Manchester United before I went to Rangers, and it was wonderful to watch Bobby close-up, even in practice matches."

And today, among the multitude of kids who dream their dreams of glory, there will be some, of whom the children of ten and fifteen years in the future will be sighing and saying . . . "I wish I could play like him."

Aberdeen's Jim Forrest admired fellow winger Bobby Charlton, the Manchester United midfield maestro

GERRY SWEENEY . . . the man who makes Morton tick. Gerry has played full-back, half-back and in the forward line, but now he has made the Morton midfield role his own. Morton certainly knew what they were doing when they signed Gerry from Celtic four years ago.

JIM COOK . . . Kilmarnock's mighty atom. An all-action, man who is at home on either wing. Freed by Hearts five years ago, the Rugby Park fans must still be wondering what went wrong at Tynecastle to let such a talented player go.

BRIAN HERON . . . started off his senior career as an outside-left with Rangers, then switched to left-back. He was transferred to Motherwell two years ago . . . and they promptly switched him back to outside-left! Brian has now made the left-wing position his own.

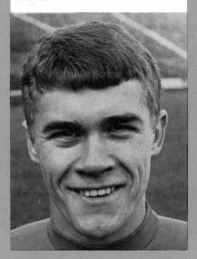

O'S WHO IN SCOTTISH FOOTBALL WH

DREW JARVIE . . . the versatile Airdrie star who is the envy of most of the big-money clubs. Drew started his career as a midfield man, but last season he developed a deadly touch in front of goal, and ended the season as one of Scotland's top scorers.

JIM PEARSON . . . St Johnstone's teenage inside-forward could emerge as one of the most dynamic babes this season. He made his debut last season at 17, and already has a tremendous understanding with Henry Hall.

ALEX REID . . . Dundee United's powerful inside-forward. Alex, freed by Rangers three years ago, forms a formidable midfield partnership with left-half Jim Henry.

SANDY JARDINE . . . one of Scotland's top attacking full-backs. Sandy, who started his career at Ibrox as wing-half or inside-forward, has gone back-wards to go forward! He started playing right-back at the beginning of last season and settled in like a veteran.

BARRIE MITCHELL . . . a £10,000 buy from Arbroath four years ago. Barrie has now settled into the Dun-fermline forward line, and is a firm favourite with the East End Park fans.

TOMMY McCULLOUCH. . . one of Scotland's most faithful club servants. Tommy has been at Shaw-field for more than a decade, and the Clyde fans are adamant that there is no safer 'keeper in the country.

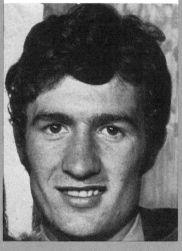

'S WHO IN SCOTTISH FOOTBALL WHO

DENIS CONNAGHAN . . . St Mirren's personality-plus goalkeeper. He had a short spell as a Celtic provisional signing before joining Saints five years ago. He also tried his luck in American soccer before returning to Paisley to be-come one of Scotland's top 'keepers.

QUINTON YOUNG . . . Ayr United's explosive right-winger who has become the target for the Scouts south of the border. Almost unstoppable when in full flight, Quinton, nicknamed 'Cutty' by the Somerset Park fans, also has a tremendous shot in either foot.

JIM STEELE . . . nicknamed 'Ironside' by the Dundee fans and anyone who has watched this mighty wing-half in action will under-stand why. Jim is a tenacious tackler and has been in trouble with referees in recent seasons but has now harnessed his explosive energy.

NOW WITH
EAST FIFE
WITH ROY
BARRY

DENIS SETTERINGTON... bought by Falkirk for £10,000 from Rangers three seasons ago. Denis, who can be used as a link-man or as striker, now forms a deadly double act with ex-Ibrox team-mate Alex Ferguson in the Brockville forward line.

ERIC CARRUTHERS ... one of the most exciting young players in the game. Eric, who made his debut in the Hearts' first team at the age of 16, is all set to make the breakthrough and win himself a permanent first team place this season.

JIMMY BONE ... Partick Thistle's human battering ram. A centre-forward of the old school who takes the shortest route to goal at every opportunity. A non-stop player who thrills the Firhill fans.

WHO IN SCOTTISH FOOTBALL WHO'S W

ARTHUR GRAHAM ... Aberdeen's young outside-left, whom the Pittodrie fans insist must play for Scotland in the future. Arthur, from Glasgow, collected the first of many honours two seasons ago when he helped the Dons beat Celtic, to win the Scottish Cup.

TOMMY CALLAGHAN ... was bought by Celtic for £35,000 from Dunfermline three years ago. The elegant mid-field man has now established himself at Parkhead after a shaky start. He is at home either at left-half or inside-forward.

JOHN HAMILTON ... the Hibs babe who has become one of Scotland's top mid-field prospects. Released five years ago by Arsenal, 'Hammy' has now re-found the sparkling form that made him a top schoolboy star.

THERE'S never a dull moment in our famous Saturday laugh-in. There's never been a sports column like it. It's talked about, fought about, loved, hated. But it's never dull. It's Sportsbag, the sports department in which the fans play a vital role.

No punches are pulled in Sportsbag. The writers are usually demanding blood — and often it's the blood (blue or green?) of Hugh Taylor, who conducts the column.

Mind you, Taylor doesn't pull any punches, either. Certainly he's never heard the old adage: "The customer is always right."

But no matter whether the subject is serious or humorous, Sportsbag is 'must' reading for every football fan on a Saturday morning.

Taylor is often battered — but he usually manages to have the last word. A cutting word, too. See for yourselves in this selection from Sportsbag. . . .

A poser from J. Finnie, Gilmerton, Edinburgh. He wrote:

"The new season has started and already we have a poser. At Tynecastle, the police made the fans drink the contents of their beer cans and put them in a bucket before gaining admission to the ground.

"But, once inside, you could buy tins of Coca-Cola. Not much of a *soft* drink if the can is used by a nut as a missile. Why bother about the beer cans?"

● *Don't you know the slogan . . . Flings go better with Coke?*

There's always mutiny in Sportsbag — and the man they want to put in irons is . . . Taylor. As this letter from T. Anstruther, of Perth,

showed:

"Although the season has hardly started, you are already showing your true colours and your bias against the little clubs.

"You idolise the big guns, such as Celtic and Rangers, and have no time for the St Johnstones, Dunfermlines, Kilmarnocks, etc.

"No wonder gates are falling outside Parkhead and Ibrox. It's the fault of you and reporters like you who bow so much to the mighty that you must lick the dust of Parkhead and Ibrox."

● *So that's what that funny taste is? I must send a note to Celtic and Rangers to make sure that when they next repair the roads outside their grounds they use Green Chartreuse and Blue Curacao, instead of tar macadam. Come off it, mate. I'm fed up with people like you blaming the Press for falling gates. Fans are not forthcoming to many grounds because of the shortcomings of the local clubs — not the reporters.*

Rangers made news when they went training on the sands of Gullane. And, of course, Sportsbag writers had plenty to say about that. For example, J. Briggs, of Dumbarton. He wrote:

"I can't understand what Rangers are trying to do with all this fierce training on the sands of Gullane. Are they trying to make the players commandos?

"When I think back on the great players I have seen, like Morton, Brown, Baxter, Gillick, Thornton, MacMillan, I wonder what they would

have said had they been taken out to train on Gullane beach. . . ."

● *"When's the next train back to Glasgow?"*

One Sportsbag client wanted football against European opposition to be banned. He was R. Armstrong, of Beith, who wrote:

"Once again we read of trouble between British and Continental opposition. I must say I am not surprised.

"Not only do players of this country play to a different set of rules from those of Europe, but the temperaments are also miles apart.

"Football in too many cases means war. I say we should stop playing these games and concentrate on British Leagues and Cups.

"Football at European level does nothing to further international relations. There is invariably trouble, and fighting at football means hatred among nations."

● *You don't have to be a foreigner to be hated by the Scots. Look how Sportsbag writers treat me . . .*

Scotland had a mixed international season — and, naturally, Sportsbag readers had plenty to say about that, too. For instance, after a poor show against Denmark, B. Feeney, of Hamilton, wrote:

"I should like to protest against the attitude of the SFA in not allowing 'Scotland the Brave' to be played before the start of the international at Hampden.

"I, for one, would rather listen to and sing our 'song' than 'God Save the Queen' which is not appropriate for

THE SPORTSBAG

the occasion, especially as royalty weren't present.

"I sincerely hope that all other true Scots — and proud to be — write in deploring the above."

● *If our team doesn't play better in the next international, I suggest that the pre-match tune should be, 'God Save Scotland'.*

All kinds of views are aired by Sportsbag writers. Here's Q. Murray, of Dundee, to say football today is too insipid. He wrote:

"You sports writers are becoming far too hypocritical. Football is a man's game, a game of physical contact. The fans appreciate the hard tackle, the fierce charge and all-out attack.

"If they didn't, why all the shouts about 'Get stuck into them' and the rest? The fans know best what they want, not you and writers like you."

● *Is that so? Are the fans also right to bawl, 'Break his leg?' If it's fighting they want not football, why don't they volunteer for service in Vietnam — or offer to do the Christmas shopping for the wife?*

...AND A GUY CALLED ROD

"*The wife is wearing them...*"

"*Look sir — you must announce your player pool, it's almost half-time...*"

"*Don't send ma pal off ref — he was only teasin' me...*"

THE TWO stars most envied by thousands of boy footballers all over Scotland are Billy McNeill, of Celtic, and John Greig, of Rangers.

They are the elite, the captains of our most influential clubs who are still Very Important People, despite the fact that the whole concept of their job has been given a managerial remould.

Their status and the inference of being inspirational remain, of course, but the giants in the thick of the action are now ordered to look more and more to the generals on the bench for guidance.

How much has the captain's job changed since George Young strode along almost as field supremo for Rangers and Scotland in the 10 years after the war?

Billy McNeill, who has become a company director and a two-car man since he first led out Celtic nine years ago, says:

"A captain still has to take responsibility. For instance, he may have to decide instantly who will take a penalty kick at a critical part of a match.

"If the recognised kicker is having a bad game I, as skipper, might ask another player to do the job.

"I regard it as my job to bring other players into the scheme of a game. I believe in shouting and making others shout as well. That is what captaincy is about.

"A captain also has to set a good example off the field as well as on it.

"When there's any dispute in the dressing-room I like to think I can step back and take an outsider's look at the problem to get it settled.

"I've also captained Scotland, but this was a different sort of job because the personnel was always changing.

"It's still a great honour to be made captain of a club like Celtic."

John Greig has been correctly described by his manager, Willie Waddell, as "a player who inspires". It was for this reason that Scot Symon first made Greig captain six years ago. Like McNeill, he is in business for himself and always presents a good image wherever he goes.

He says: "When people see me they don't say, 'there's John Greig'. They say, 'there's John Greig, captain of Rangers'.

"It's still a big thing for a player to be skipper at Ibrox. I reckon my main job is to be an encouragement to the rest of the players in every game no matter what my own form is like.

"Off the pitch it's essential

A CAPTAIN'S JOB

by Alex Cameron

to set an example to the young players. If I comport myself in the right way then they see what is expected of them.

"Some of the trickiest decisions I've had to make have concerned the tossing of coins to decide games. In Saragossa, for instance, we were level after extra-time and I called 'tails' to go into the next round.

"When I was first asked to captain Rangers I was

Celtic centre-half Billy McNeill, his arm round Billy Bremner, tries to prevent the referee from booking the little right-half in a pre-season friendly at Hampden

A captain's plea . . . Ayr United's skipper Stan Quinn queries a penalty-kick decision against his club

delighted. The position is still the same. All I want is to lead the side to more championship and Cup wins."

Managers usually prefer defenders as captains. The logic is elementary. Facing the play, it's easier to read what's happening and where mistakes are being made.

There have been exceptions. Ally McLeod led Hibs from outside-left. But, now that he is manager of Ayr United, his regular skipper is centre-half Stan Quinn.

Quinn is small but stout-hearted and a natural leader. MacLeod says: "When Stan is playing for me I know he'll make everybody else around him give 100 per cent for 90 minutes. That's what makes him such a good captain."

The player with the most unusual captain's job is John Martis, of East Fife. Because in the team with him is the manager, Pat Quinn.

But Quinn says emphatically: "When I'm playing John is still the boss on the park. He's the captain and that's that."

Nowadays would a captain dare to overrule his manager? It's unlikely. But when Bobby Moncur, of Newcastle United, captained Scotland against Denmark he said: "If I see a situation during the game which demands a change then I'd certainly make it. But, with managers sitting by the line these days it's easy to consult them during play."

Eddie Mulherron, of Clyde, found out sharply about a skipper's responsibilities when he criticised the side's tactics.

He was summoned before manager Archie Robertson and had the captaincy taken from him.

Other players find that the extra responsibility upsets their form. An example was Billy Dickson, of Kilmarnock.

Dickson, an international, found his play sagging. So, after discussing it with manager Walter McCrae, he gave up the skipper's job . . . and quickly refound the standard of play which got him to the top.

Hearts have recently tried several players as their top man . . . Alan Anderson, Jim Townsend, Eddie Thomson and Jim Cruickshank.

Cruickshank was the most unusual choice, for he is Scotland's 'keeper. However, who has a better view of play than the man between the goalposts?

Scotland's youngest top-level captain is Martin Buchan, of Aberdeen. At 21 he stepped up at Hampden to accept the Scottish Cup for the Dons.

"I was delighted to be made skipper," he says. "I'm not bothered by nerves but I am lucky to have Steve Murray playing alongside me, for he had lots of experience as Dundee's captain."

Although the importance of captains is diminishing they are certainly still much more than players who carry the ball out.

And most youngsters will continue to strive after the honour of being skipper whether it's with Rangers or Celtic or Stranraer or Brechin.

THE RETURN

SOME players have a special magic, a magic that can disappear with a transfer move to another club, a magic that is really in the minds of the fans who believe that he is *their* player . . . no matter what club he may move to.

Joe Baker has that magic, especially for Hibs fans . . . and the men who run Hibs remembered that in January 1971, when their club was going through a sad, disastrous spell.

Seldom has the proud Easter Road club been in such trouble. It fired manager Willie McFarlane, and big Dave Ewing, a former coach with Manchester City, had taken over . . . but then Hibs slid into a run of ten games without a win.

Something had to be done, the fans demanded it, the players deserved it . . . and then Hibs remembered the magic of Joe Baker, the one man with the fan-appeal and reputation to pull this tattered team together, to pull back the fans to the rapidly emptying terracings of Easter Road.

Joe Baker had been born in England, and later won international honours for his country, but he had been brought up in the football-daft atmosphere of Motherwell.

He signed for Hibs as a teenager . . . and quickly became the goal scoring hero of Scottish football.

His brother Gerry signed for St Mirren and for seasons

the biggest argument in Scottish football was who was the better centre . . . in Edinburgh there was only one answer . . . KING JOE!

But goals were, are and always will be the most valuable things in football, and any man or boy who could score as many as Joe Baker quickly became top priority in the transfer market.

And no country was more goal starved than Italy, then in the strangling grip of 'Cattenachio', a defensive system that was almost foolproof.

Milan had brought the great Jimmy Greaves to try and find a way past these human-wall defences. Turin had snapped up Denis Law for the same job . . . then in May, 1961 the Easter Road fans were shattered when Joe Baker, their King Joe, was transferred to Turin for £65,000.

However, despite a film-star-type welcome and a few golden goals, Italy was not for Joe and a year later he was brought back to Arsenal . . . for an £80,000 fee.

The travels of Joe Baker weren't over yet, the cash register hadn't rung up its last big transfer, for in 1966 Chelsea and Notts. Forest bid for the man with the golden boots and, in February

All smiles . . . that's Joe Baker and his new manager Davie Ewing as Joe signs for Hibs from Sunderland

1958 . . . young Joe Baker pictured in the epic Scottish Cup-tie against Hearts . . . Joe scored all four goals for Hibs

1971 . . . Joe makes his return to Hibs in their league match against Aberdeen, in which he scored the winning goal

of that year, Joe joined Notts. Forest.

Three years later he moved on to Sunderland.

But when clubs get themselves in trouble they usually look for a man of magic to pull them out of it. Hibs were in trouble when they remembered Joe Baker . . . but they weren't the only ones.

St Mirren were desperately fighting to get away from the threatening shadow of relegation. They remembered that Joe's brother, Gerry, had been a great hero at Paisley. They knew Joe would be the same, so they offered Sunderland £12,000 for his transfer.

Hibs immediately joined the battle for Baker and, on Jan. 14, 1971, King Joe returned to Easter Road, 10 years older, a bit heavier . . . but still with that special